TOMBS OF THE ANCIENT AMERICAS

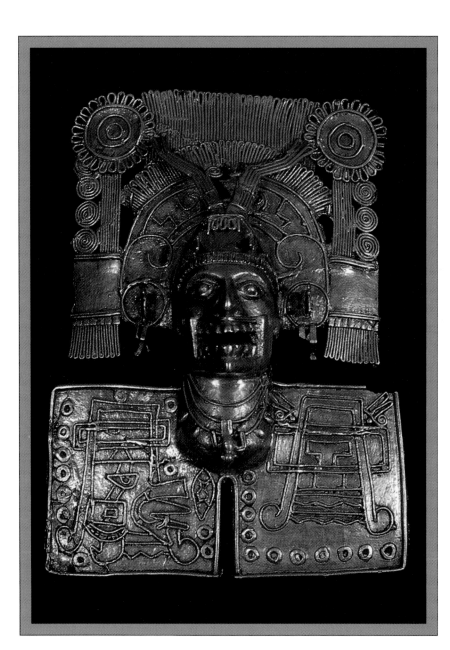

TOMBS
OF THE ANCIENT AMERICAS

Written and Illustrated
BY JEANNE BENDICK

Franklin Watts
New York / Chicago / London / Toronto / Sydney
A First Book

To Karen

Many thanks to
Dr. M. E. Moseley of the University of Florida for his
insightful comments and suggestions.

Frontis: Important Mayas wore chest ornaments called pectorals.

Cover illustration by Bob Masheris

Photographs copyright © : D. Donne Bryant/DDB Stock Photo: pp. 8, 37;
David Hiser/Photographers/Aspen: pp. 2, 28, 35, 45; Heinz Plenge/Peter
Arnold, Inc.: pp. 15, 16, 17; Nicholas deVore III/Photographers/Aspen: p. 22;
Bryon Augustin/DDB Stock Photo: p. 31; David Ryan/DDB Stock Photo: p.
38; Robert Frereck/Odyssey, Chicago: p. 40; Wadsworth Atheneum,
Hartford, CT. The Ella Gallup Sumner and Mary Catlin Sumner Collection:
p. 41; Stephen Trimble: p. 46; Tony Linck: p. 50; Ohio State Historical
Society: p. 54; Van Bucher/Photo Researchers: p. 55; Cahokia Mounds State
Historical Site, Illinois: p. 57.

Library of Congress Cataloging-in-Publication Data
Bendick, Jeanne.
Tombs of the ancient Americas / by Jeannne Bendick.
p. cm.—(A First book)
Includes bibliographical references and index.
Summary: A study of how archaeologists discover ancient burial tombs, and
how the artifacts in these tombs reveal information about such Indian cul-
tures as the Moche, Quipus, Mayas, Aztecs, and Anasazi.
ISBN 0-531-20148-1 (HC lib. bdg.)
1. Indians—Mortuary customs—Juvenile literature. 2. Tombs—America—
Juvenile literature. 3. America—Antiquities—Juvenile literature. I. Title.
II. Series.
E59.M8B45 1993
393′.1′08997—dc20
92-24546   CIP

CONTENTS

Some Mysteries of the Ancient Americas

Do you think you would be good at solving ancient mysteries?

How good a detective are you? Would you follow these clues?

A police chief in Peru raided the house of a well-known tomb robber and found a prehistoric golden head with silver and lapis eyes. Was the head a clue to a treasure the robbers had found? Would it be worth fighting gun battles over?

There was a mound near Thomas Jefferson's home in Virginia. Would you be as curious as he was to see what was in it?

A giant mound in Ohio is shaped like a snake, a quarter of a mile long. But you can only see the whole snake from the air! Who could have built it?

Why was a jade mask part of an ancient wardrobe?

Workers digging to lay electric cable in Mexico City found a huge, round stone, carved with a picture of an Aztec goddess. Could that be a clue to a lost temple?

Colored strings and knots are clues to the history of the ancient Incas. What could they mean?

7

How We Know about the Ancient Tombs

Archaeologists are scientists who study past civilizations. They study what people have left behind—buildings, objects, art, tools, bones, and graves.

They try to decode pictures, records, and writing to put together the story of how people lived, what they knew, what they believed, what they ate, how they dressed, the games they played, and whether they were peaceful or warlike. They try to date when those people lived.

Often, they have to dig out the ruins of past civilizations. Always, they try to preserve the things they find. Archaeology takes all kinds of experts—historians, *anthropologists*, *geologists*, people who know many languages, architects, chemists, engineers, and just plain careful diggers and workers.

Archaeologists try to locate the lost cities where people of the past lived and the lost tombs where they are buried. Sometimes the cities and tombs are hidden. Sometimes they are in plain view, but hard to recognize.

Archaeologists are detectives. Archaeologists solve mysteries.

Where Are the Tombs of the Ancient Americans?

They are in prehistoric ruins and graves on the two continents. In North America, they are scattered across plains and deserts, along coasts and river valleys.

In *Mesoamerica*, which is the area between the Rio Grande and Panama, they are in jungles and highlands.

In South America, they are high in the Andes Mountains and along the coasts.

Once there were no people in either North or South America. There were, however, woolly mammoths and mastodons, horses and camels, huge bisons and ground sloths. There were deer and elk, wild pigs, wolves, and bears. There were saber-toothed cats, giant armadillos, serpents, alligators, birds, and insects. There were monkeys. But no people.

There *were* humans in northeast Asia who lived by following and hunting the animals that were their food.

It was a time of Ice Ages. Great sheets of ice covered the northern parts of the Earth. So much water was frozen into ice that the ocean water level fell and land appeared where there are now seas. Then, land connected Siberia, in Asia, and Alaska, in North America. Sometimes that's called a land bridge. It was a big bridge—a thousand miles wide.

More than thirteen thousand years ago those wandering people of Asia followed the animal herds across the land bridge to North America.

They followed the animals down the grassy plains between the glaciers, and down the warmer valleys along the Rocky Mountains. They wan-

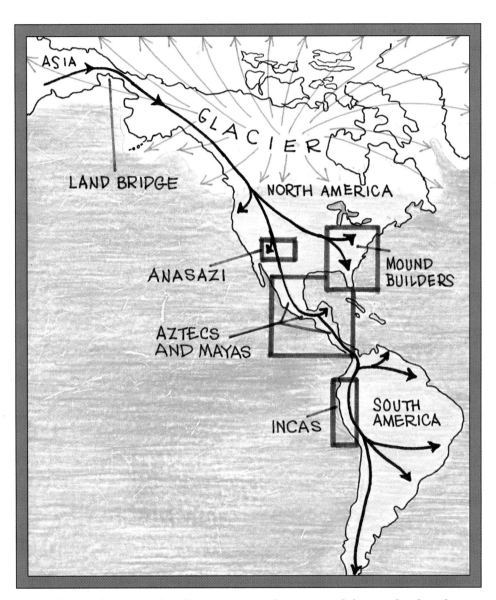

Over thousands of years, people roamed from the land bridge to the tip of South America.

dered through the forests of Canada and into the Great Plains. In each place, some stayed and some kept going. Some went into the deserts and stayed. Some crossed to the eastern woodlands and coast. Some roamed down the river valleys.

Ten thousand years ago the climate warmed. Some kinds of animals became extinct. Still, there was food everywhere for those early hunters.

Through hundreds and thousands of years the people moved on. They moved down through Mexico, down through Central America, down to South America. Some climbed up into the Andes Mountains. Some crossed into lowlands and jungles. Some kept going, all the way to the southern tip of South America.

During those thousands of years, the ways of people changed in different places. They built their houses, towns, and cities in different ways, they wore different kinds of clothes and invented different kinds of art. They imagined different gods and different ways of thinking about life and death. But everywhere, thinking about death was a big part of living.

South American Tombs

ATLANTIC
OCEAN

ONE-PERSON
TOMB

MANY INCA TOMBS
WERE SHAPED LIKE
BEEHIVES BECAUSE
PEOPLE WERE BURIED
SITTING UP.

CHAN CHAN

CUZCO

PARACAS

THE EMPIRE
OF THE INCAS

PACIFIC
OCEAN

SOUTH
AMERICA

In Peru, at a place called Sipan, nobody paid attention to the crumbling pyramid there. Nobody except the tomb robbers. For years, the robbers worked there at night, digging in the ruins and carrying off the treasure they found to sell to smugglers. (It is illegal to sell ancient treasures, regardless of whether they are found or stolen.)

In 1987, a police chief raided the house of one of the robbers and found a golden head. He called a Peruvian archaeologist named Walter Alva, who tracked down the pyramid. The tomb robbers battled to keep the pyramid.

After months of digging and fighting, Walter Alva and his crew found a royal grave that the robbers had missed. The tomb held a Lord of Sipan. He wore a golden nose ornament and a golden head dress. He had turquoise and gold necklaces, bracelets, and golden sandals, and he was lying on a bed of golden ornaments. Around him were buried people who had been sacrificed to keep him company. Even his dog was there.

Walter Alva saw that there was still another level in the pyramid, below the tomb. Could there be another tomb in the older level?

There was. This Lord's tomb was just as splendid.

Who were the people who built these pyramids and tombs?

For nine centuries, during the time when the Romans ruled in Europe and the Mediterranean, people called the *Moche* lived on the desert coastline and in the river valleys of northern Peru.

Uncovering gold and copper artifacts at a Moche tomb in Sipan

Red clay figurine jars found in Sipan grave

The Moche never invented writing. Most of what we know about them comes from their art. The Moche painted their lives on the pots they made. They painted their history and what they believed. They made portraits of the lords who ruled over them and the gods they believed in.

They wove stories into cloth, and the gold ornaments they made are so beautiful that no one, even now, has ever made any like them.

And the Moche built grand pyramids out of millions and millions of *adobe* bricks. Adobe is mud, dried in the sun. Teams of workers made the bricks and put them in place. (We know that the bricks were made by different teams, because each team put its mark on their bricks.)

All the bricks were carried by hand. The Moche didn't have carts or animals to pull loads. Nowhere in the Americas had anyone invented the wheel.

Adobe pyramid, built by the Moche at Sipan, about A.D. 200

The pyramids symbolized mountains. The lords of Moche built their palaces on the pyramids. They sacrificed prisoners there. And they were buried in the pyramids.

In about A.D. 600, the Moche civilization vanished. Maybe there was a terrible drought, or maybe the Pacific storms called El Nino destroyed their crops for years. Maybe the earthquakes that rock the Andes Mountains destroyed their towns.

Nobody knows for sure.

 ## The Mummies of Peru

In 1925, a Peruvian archaeologist named Julio Tello saw some beautiful ancient cloth for sale in a market. Because it is against the law to sell ancient treasures, he knew that grave robbers had found that cloth in a hidden place.

Tello finally traced the cloth to a half-buried city on the south coast of Peru. It was a burial place of the second century B.C.—more than two thousand years ago. Searching in the foundations of one of the buildings he found four hundred large bundles. Bundles of what? Carefully, he unwrapped them.

In each bundle there was a *mummy.* (A mummy is a dried body.) Each mummy was wrapped in layer

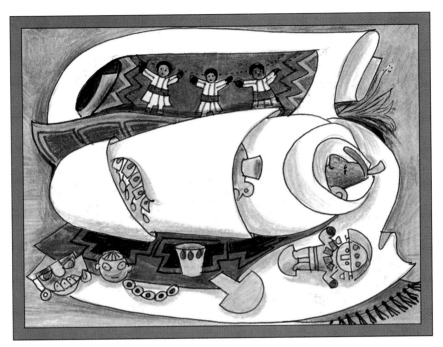

Mummy wrappings were filled with treasure.

after layer of plain cotton cloth, then in layers of the rich, beautiful material Julio Tello had first seen in the market. Between the folds of cloth were gold ornaments and pottery. There were weapons and fans made of woven cane and the feathers of tropical birds. There were many-colored ponchos, capes, and shirts. Some of the mummy wrappings had more than a hundred treasures in them. That mummy treasure place is called *Paracas*.

Quipus

The Incas had no written language. How did they keep track of the business of their huge kingdom? How did they keep track of the goods in their warehouses; of the taxes from their thousands of subjects, of the crops and the treasure?

They kept their records on bright-colored strings, with knots placed in certain places. The strings were called *quipus*. Quipu means "knots."

A quipu had a main cord, with other strings of different lengths, colors, and thickness tied to it. There were knots at different places on those different cords. All the records were kept on those strings, even the dates on which the records were made. Every knot and length and color meant something. No one has ever figured out the system.

About five hundred years ago the city of *Chan Chan* was the biggest city in South America. It was the capital city of the *Chimu* people who made beautiful woven cloth and ceramics, and worked wonderful treasures in gold and silver. The working people who made these treasures lived in tiny houses, crammed together in one part of the city.

The lords who ruled them lived apart, in walled palaces filled with treasure. The rulers claimed that their ancestors had come from two stars, while the ancestors of the common people had come from lesser stars.

When a Chimu ruler died, his palace, with all its treasure, was sealed off to become his tomb. Many young women were sacrificed to join him in his next life. Then a new ruler would begin building a new palace, which was sealed off when he died. Gradually, Chan Chan became a huge *necropolis*, or a city of the dead.

The Chimu were defeated by the Incas, who built and ruled over an immense mountain kingdom which they called, "The Land of the Four Quarters." All the parts of the kingdom were connected by 19,000 miles (30,400 km) of roads. Runners carried

Cuzco, great city of the Incas

goods and messages up and down the mountains from their great stone city, Cuzco, to all the parts of the country.

The Incas had no carts or horses. Sometimes they used llamas—animals that are members of the camel family. But llamas aren't fast. And they can't carry big loads. Even a person is too heavy.

The Inca ruler was called "The Inca." The Spanish conquerors saw the last Inca, and described him. "He rode on a throne made of solid gold, carried by hundreds of his people. The throne was lined with the feathers of brilliant tropical birds and around his neck was a collar of huge emeralds."

 ## What the Incas Believed

They believed that they were under the protection of Inti, the sun god, and that their rulers, The Incas, were descended from him. Being a god, The Inca could not die. Worshipping the royal mummy kept his spirit alive.

When an Inca ruler passed on, all his lands and treasures, buildings, and servants, were still the property of the royal mummy. It was the job of his descendants to maintain his household and his

The Mummy-King attended all festivals.

mummy and to serve the mummy just as if he were alive.

Rulers were never considered dead. There were dances and festivals in the courts and the royal mummies visited one another to enjoy them. They attended every major ceremony, sitting in Cuzco's grand plaza.

The nobles owned everything in the Kingdom of the Four Quarters—all the treasure, the crops, the grand buildings. Ordinary people were forbidden to own anything but their small houses and what they needed for their everyday lives.

Whether they were rich or poor, the Incas paid a lot of attention to the people who died. Sometimes they were seated in high mountain places with their favorite things around them. There, the cold and wind made mummies of them. But usually mummies were placed in above-ground tombs made of stone or clay. They were seated upright, wrapped in layers of beautiful cloth. Rich people were buried with treasure. Working people were buried with their tools. Fishermen had nets. Weavers had cotton, ready to weave. Potters had clay so they could make pots. And they all had food, so they would not go hungry in the next world.

Mesoamerican Tombs

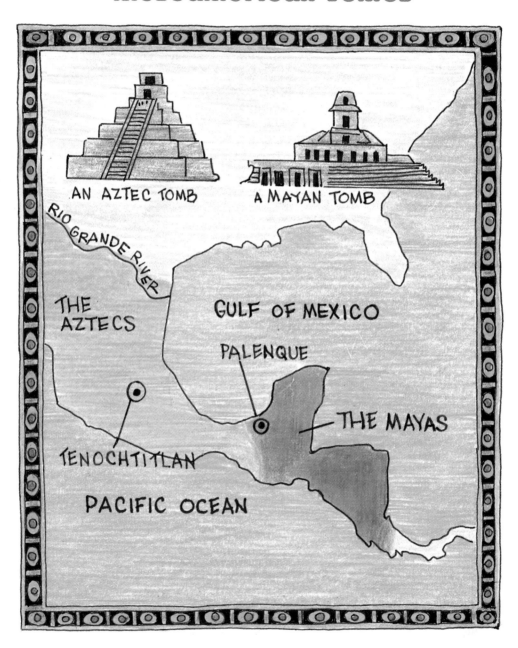

AN AZTEC TOMB

A MAYAN TOMB

RIO GRANDE RIVER

THE AZTECS

GULF OF MEXICO

PALENQUE

TENOCHTITLAN

THE MAYAS

PACIFIC OCEAN

In southern Mexico, in a steamy, tropical jungle about 50 miles (80 km) from the Gulf of Mexico, there is an ancient city of the Mayans called *Palenque*. People settled there before the year A.D. 200, and a few years later they began building their city. They built houses, palaces, ball courts, and temples. The most important building was a great pyramid with a grand staircase and a four-story tower.

In about the year A.D. 800, the people of Palenque abandoned their city and moved away. The jungle crept in and over the city, hiding it. The pyramid fell into ruins. Some small villages grew up nearby but the farmers there forgot that there ever was a great city.

Almost a thousand years later, a Spanish priest discovered the ruins and thought there might be treasure there. Through the years he and some of the local Indians worked to uncover the ruins, which showed a past so grand that archaeologists came from many places to look at them. They all had theories about the builders. No one even considered that ancestors of the nearby Indians could have build such a city.

The ruins of the palace at Palenque

Could the Greeks or the Romans have discovered America and settled there long before the Spanish came? Maybe the city was theirs.

Had the place been build by refugees from the lost continent of Atlantis? Legends said that the buildings in Atlantis had been wonderful.

One authority said that the city must have been a colony of ancient Egypt. Look at that pyramid!

Still another expert was sure that it had been built by an ancient Chinese dynasty. Wasn't that a pagoda on top?

Over the years the digging continued and so did the arguments.

Around 1949, Albert Ruz, director of the Mexican Institute of Anthropology and History, decided to excavate the floor of the Temple. He thought there might be an older building under it because the Mayas often build one pyramid over another. Where to begin? Looking closely at the floor of an inner room he saw one stone that seemed a little different.

There was a double row of holes in that stone. Could they be a place for fingers?

Yes! He lifted the stone. What was under it?

After digging carefully for a few days, Ruz and his crew uncovered a step, then another and another. It was a secret staircase leading down into the pyramid.

Archaeology takes a lot of patience. It took years to clear the staircase because the builders had blocked it all along the way to protect against tomb robbers.

There were forty-five steps, then a U turn, then twenty-one steps more.

At the bottom of the steps there was a box with three pottery dishes, two shells with semi-precious stones, seven jade beads, some jade ear plugs, and a beautiful pearl.

Three years after he began his dig, Ruz and his team came to a triangular slab of stone, 6 feet (1.8 m) high. It looked like a door. In front of the door were six skeletons.

It took two days for the crew to move the slab enough for Ruz to slide through, into a room cut out of the pyramid rock. The room was almost filled with a huge block of stone. Carved on the lid was an important-looking man falling down through the branches of a tree.

The next question was, how could they lift the huge, heavy lid of the *sarcophagus*? (A sarcophagus is a stone coffin.)

Ruz and his team went out into the forest and cut down big trees. They made the trunks into levers, dragged them back into the pyramid and

Replica of King Pacal's sarcophagus

down the steps. Even with the levers, it took days to lift the lid.

There was a very tall skeleton inside. Its head was covered by a jade mask. Its body was draped with pounds of jade—necklaces, pendants, bracelets, rings. Carved jade statues of gods were alongside. Who had been buried in such splendor?

Was it a foreigner who had been thought to be a god?

Now, because archaeologists can read most of the records of the Mayas, they know that the royal person was Lord Jaguar Pacal, king of Palenque from A.D. 615 to 683. His tomb was the grandest ever to be found in the Americas.

 ## What the Mayas Believed

The Mayas believed that there were three levels to the universe. The Upperworld was the top layer—the heavens, where supernatural beings lived.

The Middleworld was where the humans lived. The Middleworld only existed because the king, standing on a pyramid, brought it into being.

Below that was the Underworld, where the souls of the dead were.

The World Tree. The gods live on top, in the sky.
Humans live in the middle. The dead are underground.

All the worlds were connected by the World Tree. Its roots were in the Underworld, its trunk was in the Middleworld, and its branches were in the Upperworld. Gods and souls of the dead could pass from level to level through the tree.

The Mayas believed that time went in a circle and that people returned to the same time and space when they completed the circle. They had several calendars, and they used them all so they could do the proper things on the proper days. They believed that different gods, some good, some bad, took over different times of the day and were responsible for the good and bad things that happened.

The Mayas believed that their gods wanted blood—sometimes a little, sometimes a lot. So they sacrificed enemies, captives, and even the losers of the ball games they played in the great ball courts that were a part of every plaza.

The Mayas had a fine irrigation system. Farmers raised enough food to feed the people in the big Maya cities. Why were those cities abandoned? Maybe the farmers got tired of feeding so many people who didn't grow anything. Nobody knows for sure.

The Written Records of the Mayas

The Mayas lived in what is now Mexico and Guatemala. Their civilization seemed to start about 292. It collapsed about 500 years later.

The Mayas left a lot of information about themselves in their books, called *codices*. Some codices are picture books, written on folded strips of bark or deer skin. There are also painted codices on walls and ceramics. There are carved pictures and symbols called *glyphs* on walls and pillars. The pillars are called *steles*.

A Mayan Stella

The records tell about Mayan history, geography, astronomy, religion, ancestors, their calendar, and legend of heroes.

The Mayans had a fine number system. They knew how to use zero before the Europeans did. They could write any number with only three symbols. Mayan numerals help archaeologists to date their civilization.

MAYAN NUMBER SYMBOLS - ● ━ ⬭

●	●●	●●●	●●●●	━	━	━	━	━	━
1	2	3	4	5	6	7	8	9	10

BUT WHAT WAS THIS? ⬭

IT WAS USED LIKE THIS: 20   200

The Aztecs: The Great Temple of Tenochtitlan

In the winter of 1978, workers who were digging a hole to install an electric cable near the cathedral in Mexico City struck the top of a big stone, 15 feet (4.6m) below the street. They dug out the stone which was almost eleven feet across. On the stone was a carving of the *Aztec* moon goddess.

Everybody knew that this was something important. Was it possible that here, under the street, was the lost Great Temple of the Aztecs? Could this have been the center of the capital city of the Aztecs?

Directed by the archaeologist Matos Moctezuma the digging went on for five years. It was the Great Temple, and it held one discovery after another. (Moctezuma had the same name as the Aztec emperor who was conquered by Cortes in 1519.)

There wasn't just one temple—there were six, one inside the other. Each pyramid had its own shrines and sculptures, offerings to the gods, and tribute from captives. The Great Temple was a double pyramid, with a double flight of steps leading to two temples, one for the god of sun and one for water and the rain god.

Quetzalcoatl was the most important Aztec god.

Another pyramid belonged to the main Aztec god, *Quetzalcoatl,* the feathered serpent who was god of the wind. Some of the pyramids of the lost temples are part of the subway stations in Mexico City today.

This Aztec altar was uncovered when the
Metro (subway) was being built in
Mexico City. It's in a station.

Nobody knows for sure where the Aztecs came from, because they destroyed the records of everyone that they conquered. Their own legend says that in the year 1193 they left Aztlan, a place somewhere north or west of Mexico and finally built their capital on an island in Lake Texcoco about 1315. In less than two hundred years, they ruled most of Mexico. Then, in 1520, their empire was destroyed by the Spanish conquerors.

 ## What the Aztecs Believed

They believed that they were the chosen people of the sun, and that it was their duty to supply the sun with the food it needed—sacrificed humans. They believed that without human sacrifice there would be no earth, no life, no future.

The Aztecs believed that the world had been created and destroyed four times, and their world was the fifth. They called their kingdom the World of the Fifth Sun. They believed that this world, too, would be destroyed and only victims sacrificed to their gods could save it.

These sacrifices were made at the Great Temple, which they thought was the center of the universe. Below the platform on which the temple was built

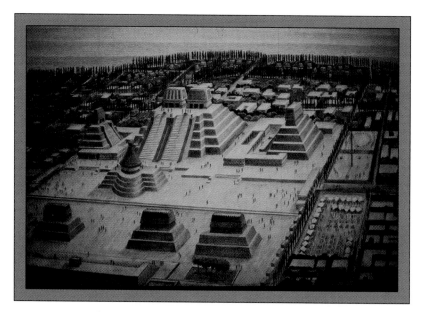

Tenochtitlan was the Aztec capital.

was the underworld. Above the temple lived the gods. The Aztecs thought the universe was surrounded by a ring of water. They could see this was true; their city, *Tenochtitlan,* was built on an island in a great lake.

At the time the Spanish landed in Mesoamerica, the Aztec empire stretched from the Gulf of Mexico to the Pacific Ocean. The emperor Moctezuma surrendered his kingdom to Cortes because he mistakenly believed Cortes was the god Quetzalcoatl returning from heaven. An Aztec prophesy had foretold that.

The battle between Cortez and the Aztecs
at one of the great pyramids.

North American Tombs

ADENAS AND HOPEWELLS   MISSISSIPPIANS

THE MOUND BUILDERS BUILT
MOUNDS OF MANY SHAPES

CANADA

MESA VERDE

CASA
MALPAIS

CHACO

MEXICO

● ADENAS
● HOPEWELLS
● MISSISSIPPIANS
● ANASAZI

The Seven Cities of Cibola

The Spanish conquerors who came to Meso-america believed in a legend that told about seven cities in the north, where the streets and buildings were gold and silver, and all the people were dressed in precious metal.

An expedition, headed by the Spanish explorer Coronado marched north across the deserts of the American southwest and found only adobe villages of crowded houses. No great cities, no gold, no treasure.

 # The Tomb of the Mogollon

About nine hundred years ago, in a place called Casa Malpais, some people called the *Mogollon* built their pueblo village. *Pueblo* is a Spanish word that means a lot of things together. It means people + settlement + village + buildings of several stories. The Mogollon lived in their pueblo for a hundred years, then left. No one knows why. In 1991, some archaeologists who were exploring Casa Malpais squeezed through a crack in the rock where the village was, and found themselves in acres of huge caves. They walked through cave after cave. All around them were the skeletons of hundreds of Mogollons. The caves were their tomb. Some were buried under piles of stones. Some were in stone coffins. Some lay in shelves, cut out of the cave walls. Tombs like this are called *catacombs*. The Mogollon tombs are the only catacombs ever found in North America.

 ## The Anasazi

About three thousand years ago the American Indians who lived in the deserts of the Southwest stopped being hunters and gatherers and learned to grow *maize*. (The people south of them, in Mexico, had been farming maize for thousands of years.)

When people become farmers they can stop wandering. First, those people lived in caves in the cliffs. Then they began building pueblos. Nobody knows what those people called themselves—they had no written language. The Navajos, who came later, call them *Anasazi*, which means "enemy ancestors." Others call them just "the ancient ones."

The Anasazi built their cities in the cliffs or at cliff bases. They farmed the *mesas*, the flat lands

The cliff palace ruins at Mesa Verde

A kiva at Pueblo Bonito

on the cliff tops. They made baskets, pottery, and jewelry. They built roads and traded with Mexico. Suddenly, about eight hundred years ago, they moved out of their cities. Nobody knows why, or what happened to them.

The cities are still there. Some look like castles in the cliffs. Some look like blocks of apartment houses. An important part of every settlement was a *kiva*. A kiva is a round room, partly underground. A ladder or steps from the roof goes down into the kiva. The kiva represented the underworld from which humans climbed up to live on earth.

We don't really know what the Anasazi believed or what ceremonies went on in the kivas, but only men and boys were allowed there. The modern Pueblo Indians seem to be descendants of the Anasazi. They still use kivas.

 ## What the Pueblo People Believed

Because they had no written language, nobody knows for sure what the ancient American Indians believed. But this is what their descendants think.

They believed in a Creator of all life, and they respected all life. They believed that life should be lived in a natural way and that five things were necessary to their lives—the sun, the earth, water, fire, and corn and the seeds of growing things.

They believed in their *shaman*, a wise man who could read the stars, tell them when to plant, cure illness, and pass along advice from the spirits.

They believed that their kivas—half below and half above ground—were links with the spirit world.

The ancient American Indians of the southwest did believe in a life after death. They buried some of their dead under the floors of their houses, with things they might need in that afterlife.

Archaeologists have found other, mysterious graves. Some have many skulls in them, but no bodies. Some have bodies but no skulls. The skulls and the bodies don't match. Some graves have only hands. One has pairs of hands with a sandal in each hand.

In the biggest Anasazi settlements, no large burial places or tombs have ever been found. Could they be in secret caves, like the Mogollons? It's still a mystery.

 ## The Mound Builders

From the journals of Meriwether Lewis and William Clark, who were sent by President Thomas Jefferson, to explore America west of the Mississippi River:

24 August, Friday, 1804
In a northerly direction from the Mouth of this Creek a high Hill is situated, and appears of a Conic form and by the nations of Indians in this quarter is Suppose to be the residence of Deavels. . . . No Consideration is Sufficient to induce them to approach the hill.

About three thousand years ago, even before the great civilizations of the other Americas, American Indians in the central and southeastern United States began to bury their dead in a special way.

At first, they simply covered them with mounds of earth. Later, they began to include food and weapons. They added ornaments that were specially made to be buried with the dead.

Over time the mounds became bigger and bigger. Some were so big that it must have taken thousands of people years to make them, carrying earth basket by basket. More and more bodies were added. The goods and ornaments in the mounds got more elaborate.

In some places, the dead were cremated before they were buried. The bones were painted red, and red powder was sprinkled over everything. Sometimes the ornaments that were buried with them were broken first or burned.

Nobody knows why people did those things. Nobody knows what they believed, except that death was very important to them. They invented ways to feel comfortable about dying. They tried to protect the dead and provide for them by giving them clothes, food, weapons, and treasure to use wherever they were going. The mound builders

The Great Serpent Mound

buried their dead this way for seventeen hundred years.

Some mounds are huge. Some are shaped like immense bears of lizards. Others are shaped like people or big birds with their wings outstretched. The Great Serpent mound in Ohio, stretches a quarter of a mile (402 m) —as long as eighteen football fields—from its tail to its jaws, which hold what seems to be a giant egg.

Nobody knows how the mound builders made those huge, perfect shapes, which can't really be seen except from the air. They must have had mathematicians or engineers to make the plans. There must have been rulers to order the mounds. There certainly were many workers who did the carrying and building.

When early settlers from Europe came across those mounds, they thought that they must have been built by some mysterious superpeople who had settled in the country some long past time.

The first explorers to see the mounds didn't think that, because in some places the mound builders were still at work. The Spanish explorer, Hernando de Soto, saw mounds when he landed in Florida in 1539. One account says, "He opened a large temple in the woods, in which were buried the chiefs of the country and took from it a quantity of pearls."

Thomas Jefferson was another mound explorer. In 1781, he became curious about a mound near his home at Monticello, Virginia. He wondered if it could be an "Indian monument" built to honor the dead. Jefferson found a great number of bones in "confused condition." Skulls were together in one layer. Other bones were together in different layers. Jefferson estimated that there were about nine hundred people buried in the mound. Many scholars say that Thomas Jefferson was the first American archaeologist.

Mounds were built by different groups of American Indians at different times and for different reasons. We don't know what the mound builders believed or even what they called themselves. North American archaeology is different from archaeology anywhere else because those American Indians had no written language.

There seem to have been three different groups of mound builders.

Usually they are named for the places where their mounds were first found. The *Adenas* were named after an estate in Ohio. The Adenas built from about twenty-five hundred years ago to about eighteen hundred years ago. Some people think they might have come from Mexico, because some

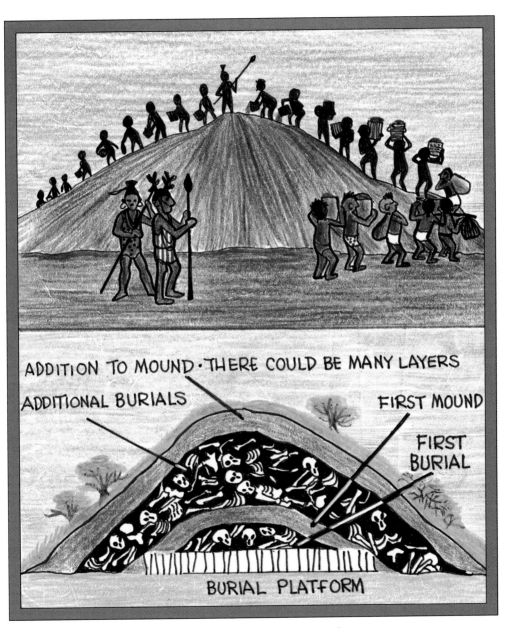

ADDITION TO MOUND·THERE COULD BE MANY LAYERS

ADDITIONAL BURIALS

FIRST MOUND

FIRST BURIAL

BURIAL PLATFORM

Mounds usually had many layers

An Adenas pipe

of the objects found in their tombs look like carvings of the Olmecs, an ancient Mexican people.

Many Adena mounds were splendid. At first, the Adenas were buried in log tombs. Useful objects were buried with them, along with other possessions for them to enjoy—copper beads and bracelets, shell beads, masks, wonderfully carved stone pipes, and ornaments cut from mica.

Small, engraved stone tablets were put in their hands. Other bodies were added, then the shelter was burned down and covered with earth. Over fifty or a hundred years the mounds grew bigger and bigger.

After about seven hundred years, the Adenas seemed to disappear. Nobody knows what happened to them.

The next mound builders are called the *Hopewells*, after Captain M.C. Hopewell, on whose Ohio farm a group of thirty mounds was found.

Hopewell mounds at Mound City, Ohio

The lives of the Hopewells centered around death. Most of the wealth of the people went into the mounds of their rulers. The Hopewells must have traded all across the continent for their treasures. Hopewell mounds had shells, alligator and shark teeth from the Gulf of Mexico, and other shells from the Atlantic Ocean. They had copper from Lake Superior and grizzly bear teeth from the Rocky Mountains. They had obsidian from the west, mica from the Carolinas, and gallons of pearls. One chief was buried on a platform of twenty thousand shell beads. He was surrounded by the skeletons of many relatives sacrificed with him.

After about six hundred years the Hopewells vanished, just as the Adenas had. Nobody knows why. Maybe the ordinary people got tired of putting everything they made into the tombs of the people who ruled them. Grass and trees grew over the mounds and they became part of the landscape.

The last of the mound builders are called the *Mississippians*, and their great mound is at a place in Illinois where many smaller rivers join at the Mississippi. The place is called *Cahokia* and the mound is called Monks Mound. It is the biggest earthen building in the Americas. Archaeologists say it took about three hundred years to build. Monks Mound wasn't a tomb—it had a temple on

Monks Mound at Cahokia

top. But not far away are the tombs of the nobles of the time, as usual, buried in splendor.

The Mississippians built flat-topped pyramids with temples on top. Their customs seemed like those of the Mayas. They practiced human sacrifice. Some people think that they were people from the coast of Mexico who came by sea, across the Gulf of Mexico.

The mounds are still there—more than one hundred thousand of them in the United States.

The cliff cities are still there.

So are the pyramids in Mesoamerica and South America.

The treasures from those places are in many museums.

There are mysteries that have not been solved.

Nobody really knows why people in all the Americas abandoned their cities so suddenly.

Nobody has learned to read all the glyphs and codices of the Mayas and the Aztecs.

Nobody has figured out a quipu.

Nobody knows how the Incas moved such large stones up the mountains to build their cities.

Nobody knows where all the mounds are. Are there small hills where you live? Could they be mounds?

Do you think that someday you might solve some of the mysteries?

Glossary

Adenas (ah-DEEN-as). The oldest known Mound Builders of North America.

Adobe (ah-DOUGH-be). Mud, dried in the sun.

Anasazi (an-a-SAZZ-i). The ancient Indians of the American southwest.

Anthropologist. A scientist who studies the development, beliefs and customs of people.

Archaeologist (ark-EE-OL-o-gist). A scientist who studies past civilizations.

Aztecs (AZ-TECKS). The ancient people of northern Mexico.

Cahokia (ca-HO-KEY-a). The place where Monks Mound, the great mound of the Mississippian culture, is located.

Catacombs (CAT-a-COMBS). Cemetery caves.

Chan Chan. In ancient times, the biggest city in South America.

Chimu (she-MU). The people who lived in Chan Chan.

Codices (KO-di-SEES). The painted or carved picture records of the Mayas.

Geologist. A scientist who studies the earth and how it changes.

Glyphs (gliffs). Carved pictures and symbols.

Hopewells. Ancient Mound Builders of central United States.

Incas (inkas). The people who built, ruled, and lived in the most powerful kingdom of ancient South America.

Kiva (KEY-va). A round, partly underground ceremonial room of American Indians.

Maya (MAY-a). The ancient people of southern Mexico and Guatemala.

Mesas (MAY-sas). Flat lands on the tops of cliffs.

Mesoamerica (MEZZ-O-america). The area between the Rio Grande and Panama.

Mississippians. Last of the Mound Builders of central and southern United States.

Moche (MO-che). Ancient desert people of northern Peru.

Mocteuzuma (mock-te-ZOOM-a). The Aztec emperor who was conquered by Cortes. Also the archeologist who uncovered their Great Temple.

Mogollon (MUG-gy-OWN). Early Pueblo people of the American southwest.

Mummy. A dried body.

Necropolis (neh-CROP-o-lis). A city of the dead.

Palenque (pal-ENK). One of the great Mayan cities.

Pueblo (PWEB-lo). The adobe settlements and buildings of the American southwest.

Quetzalcoatl (ket-sal-coh-AT-l). The main Aztec god.

Quipu (KEY-pu). Knotted strings on which the Incas kept their records.

Sarcophagus (sar-COFF-a-gus). A stone coffin.

Shaman (SHAY-man). A wise man, sometimes doing magic.

Steles (STEEL-ez). Carved pillars.

Tenochtitlan (te-nock-tit-LAN). The Great Temple of the Aztecs.

For Further Reading

Gallant, Roy. *Ancient Indians: The First Americans.* Hillside, NJ: Enslow Publishers, 1989.

Greene, Jacqueline D. *The Maya.* New York: Franklin Watts, 1992.

Hallett, Bill & Jane. *Pueblo Indians of New Mexico: Activities & Adventures for Kids.* Tucson, AZ: Look & See Publishers, 1992.

Hoyt-Goldsmith, Diane. *Pueblo Storyteller.* New York: Holiday House, 1991.

Marrin, Alfred. *Inca & Spaniard: Pizarro & the Conquest of Peru.* New York: Macmillan, 1989.

Marrin, Alfred. *Aztecs & Spaniards: Cortes & the Conquest of Mexico.* New York: Macmillan, 1989.

Newman, Shirlee P. *The Incas.* New York: Franklin Watts, 1992.

Shepherd, Donna Walsh. *The Aztecs.* New York: Franklin Watts, 1992.

Snow, Dean R. *Archaeology of North America.* New York: Chelsea House, 1989.

Tannenbaum, Beulah & Harold E. *Science of the Early American Indians.* New York: Franklin Watts, 1988.

Trout, Lawana. *Maya.* New York: Chelsea House, 1989.

Index

About the Author

Jeanne Bendick is a prolific, award-winning writer and illustrator of books for children. Her association with Franklin Watts dates back to the 1950s; in 1953 she won the Spring Book Festival 8–12 Honor for The First Book of Space Travel. Among her many other awards, Ms. Bendick has been honored by the New York Academy of Sciences (1974) and the American Nature Study Society's Eva L. Gordon Award (1985).

Readers of *Tombs of the Ancient Americas* will likely be interested in Jeanne Bendick's previous First Book, *Egyptian Tombs*.